Cabot's
Bad Habit

by J. C. Cunningham
illustrations by Scott Ross

Harcourt Brace & Company

Orlando Atlanta Austin Boston San Francisco Chicago Dallas New York Toronto London

Once upon a time, there was a little dragon—Cabot Dragon.

2

Cabot Dragon had a bad habit.

Cabot saw a woman.

Cabot yelled, "I'm

a big, bad dragon!"

The woman ran away.

4

Cabot saw a cabin.

Cabot yelled, "I'm

a big, bad dragon!"

Cabot's bad habit went on. Then Mother Dragon saw Cabot's bad habit.

"Cabot Dragon!" she yelled. "You are a little dragon with a big, bad habit!"

Cabot—the big, bad
dragon—had to go to
his room!